HYMNS WITH A TOUCH OF JAZZ

CONTENTS

3 **COME, THOU FOUNT OF EVERY BLESSING**

6 **COME, THOU LONG-EXPECTED JESUS**

9 **FAIREST LORD JESUS**

12 **GOD WILL TAKE CARE OF YOU**

14 **I LOVE TO TELL THE STORY**

17 **I'VE GOT PEACE LIKE A RIVER**

20 **JESUS IS ALL THE WORLD TO ME**

26 **JESUS, THE VERY THOUGHT OF THEE**

23 **JUST A CLOSER WALK WITH THEE**

30 **PRAISE TO THE LORD, THE ALMIGHTY**

33 **SAVIOR, LIKE A SHEPHERD LEAD US**

36 **SOFTLY AND TENDERLY**

41 **STAND UP, STAND UP FOR JESUS**

44 **THIS IS MY FATHER'S WORLD**

46 **WHAT A FRIEND WE HAVE IN JESUS**

— PIANO LEVEL —
LATE INTERMEDIATE/EARLY ADVANCED

ISBN 978-0-634-07383-0

HAL•LEONARD®
CORPORATION
7777 W. BLUEMOUND RD. P.O. BOX 13819 MILWAUKEE, WI 53213

Visit Hal Leonard Online at
www.halleonard.com

Visit Phillip at
www.phillipkeveren.com

PREFACE

The enduring beauty of hymns is remarkable. These songs have been arranged in countless ways through the years, and no matter the style, they provide inspiration to all who hear them. In this collection, we blend these classic melodies with the rich harmonies and syncopated rhythms of the jazz tradition.

"What a Friend We Have in Jesus" is my mother's favorite hymn, so this setting is dedicated to her. We are currently celebrating her renewed health following a major surgery. What a Friend indeed!

Sincerely,
Phillip Keveren

BIOGRAPHY

Phillip Keveren, a multi-talented keyboard artist and composer, has composed original works in a variety of genres from piano solo to symphonic orchestra. Mr. Keveren gives frequent concerts and workshops for teachers and their students in the United States, Canada, Europe, and Asia. Mr. Keveren holds a B.M. in composition from California State University Northridge and a M.M. in composition from the University of Southern California.

COME, THOU FOUNT OF EVERY BLESSING

Words by ROBERT ROBINSON
Music from *The Sacred Harp*
Arranged by Phillip Keveren

Rubato, expressively

COME, THOU LONG-EXPECTED JESUS

Words by CHARLES WESLEY
Music by ROWLAND HUGH PRICHARD
Arranged by Phillip Keveren

Briskly

8

D.C. al Coda

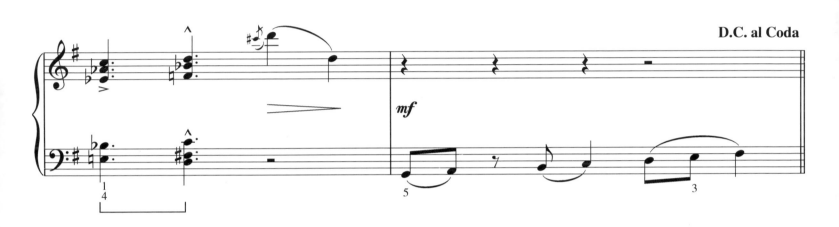

CODA

FAIREST LORD JESUS

Words from *Munster Gesangbuch*
Music from *Schlesische Volkslieder*
Arranged by Phillip Keveren

Slowly, freely

GOD WILL TAKE CARE OF YOU

Words by CIVILLA D. MARTIN
Music by W. STILLMAN MARTIN
Arranged by Phillip Keveren

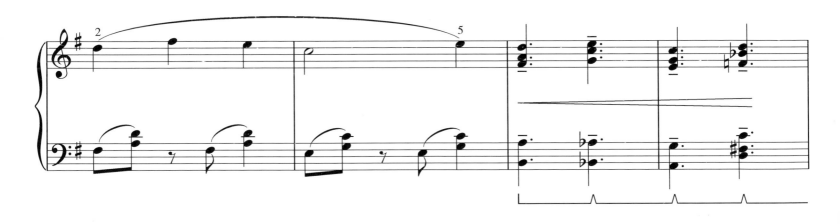

I LOVE TO TELL THE STORY

Words by A. CATHERINE HANKEY
Music by WILLIAM G. FISCHER
Arranged by Phillip Keveren

I'VE GOT PEACE LIKE A RIVER

Traditional
Arranged by Phillip Keveren

Serenely

JESUS IS ALL THE WORLD TO ME

Words and Music by WILL L. THOMPSON
Arranged by Phillip Keveren

JUST A CLOSER WALK WITH THEE

Traditional
Arranged by Phillip Keveren

Moderate Swing

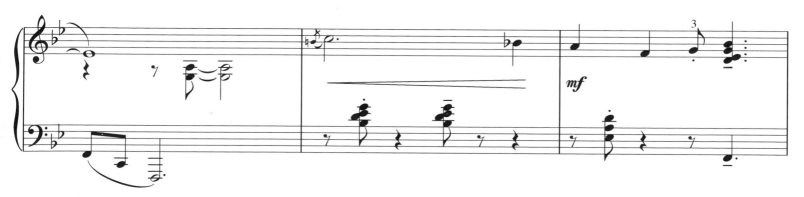

JESUS, THE VERY THOUGHT OF THEE

Words attributed to BERNARD OF CLAIRVAUX
Music by JOHN BACCHUS DYKES
Arranged by Phillip Keveren

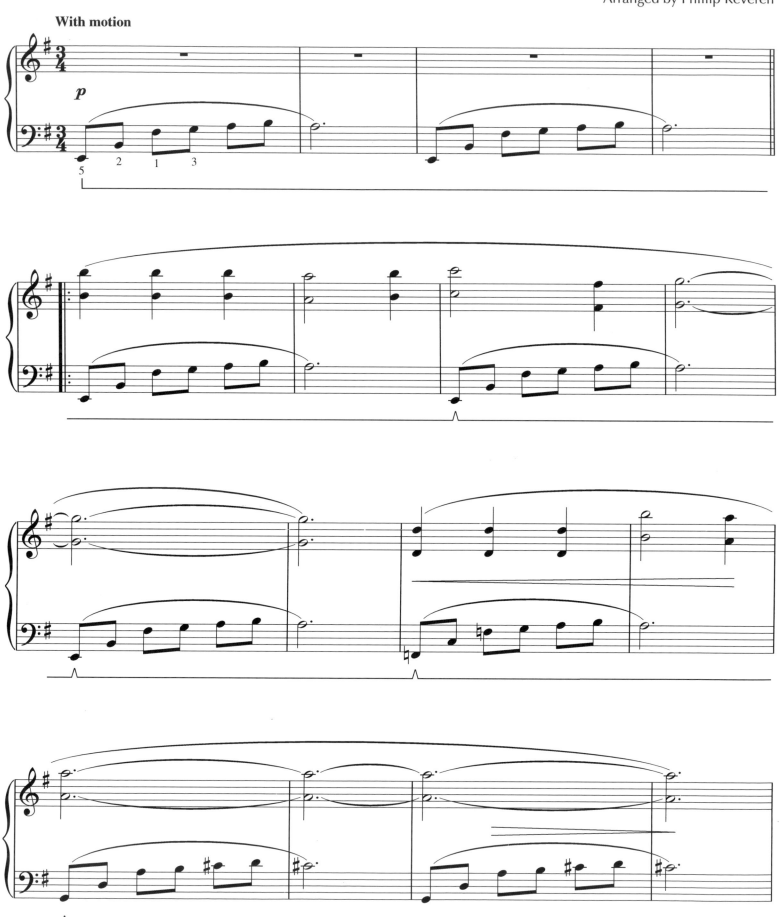

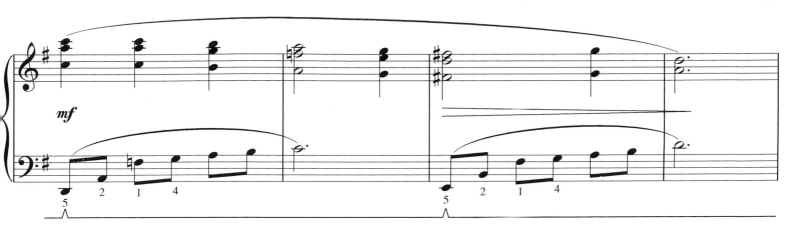

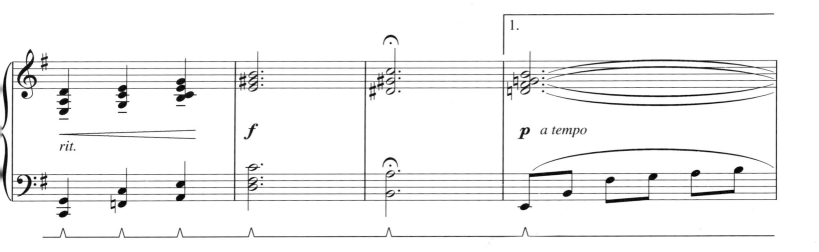

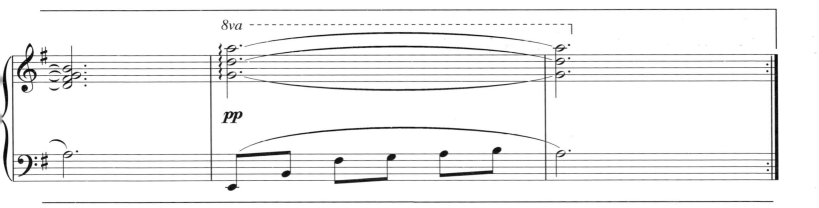

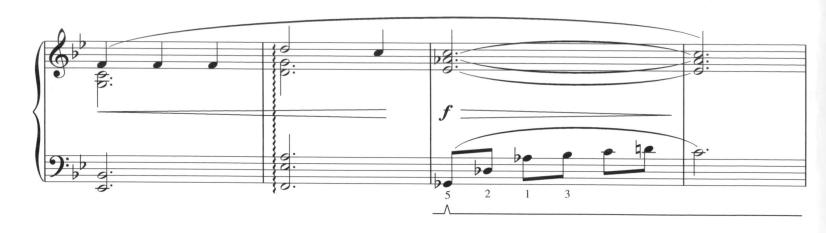

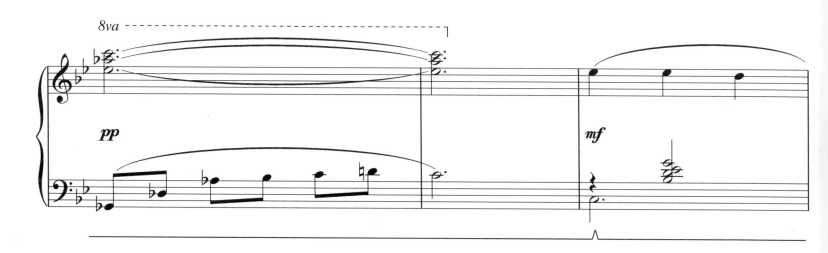

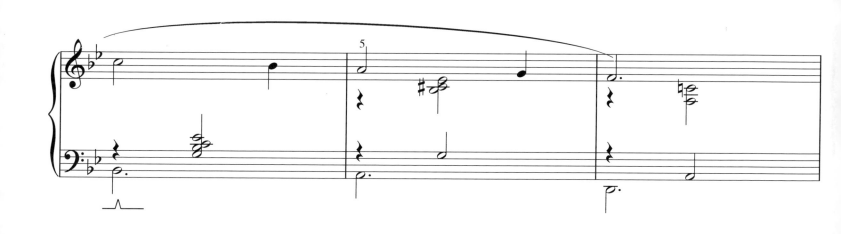

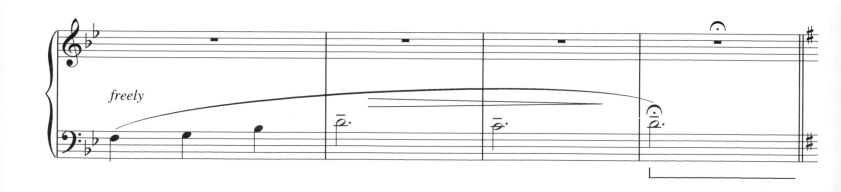

Tempo I

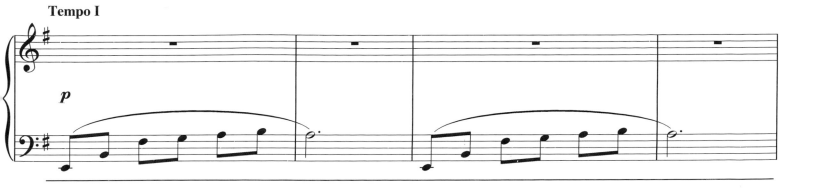

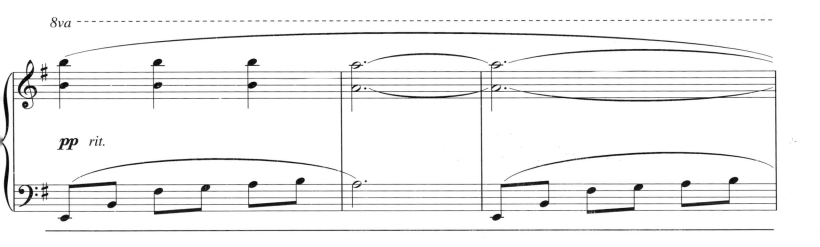

PRAISE TO THE LORD, THE ALMIGHTY

Words by JOACHIM NEANDER
Music from *Erneuerten Gesangbuch*
Arranged by Phillip Keveren

SAVIOR, LIKE A SHEPHERD LEAD US

Words from *Hymns For The Young*
Attributed to DOROTHY A. THRUPP
Music by WILLIAM B. BRADBURY
Arranged by Phillip Keveren

SOFTLY AND TENDERLY

Words and Music by
WILL L. THOMPSON
Arranged by Phillip Keveren

STAND UP, STAND UP FOR JESUS

Words by GEORGE DUFFIELD, JR.
Music by GEORGE J. WEBB
Arranged by Phillip Keveren

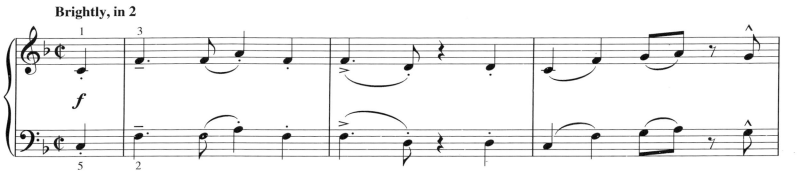

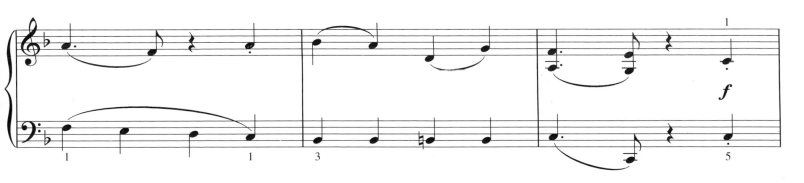

THIS IS MY FATHER'S WORLD

Words by MALTBIE D. BABCOCK
Music by FRANKLIN L. SHEPPARD
Arranged by Phillip Keveren

WHAT A FRIEND WE HAVE IN JESUS

Words by JOSEPH M. SCRIVEN
Music by CHARLES C. CONVERSE
Arranged by Phillip Keveren

Slowly, with tenderness